W9-AXA-899

J $13.27
636
He   Henderson, Kathy
              I can be a rancher

DATE DUE

AP 25'91	NO 19'92	NOV 17 '94	JUN 01 '98
JY 3'01	MR 1'93	DEC 03 '94	JUL 13 '98
AG 12'91	AP 8'93	MAY 02 '95	JUL 27 '98
SE 3'91	JE 8'93	JUL 10 '95	OCT 13 '9
SE 25'91	OC 21'03	OCT 19 '95	NOV 27 '9
	DEC 20 '93	JUL 05 '96	FEB 02 '9
	JAN 27 '94	AUG 01 '96	MR 29 '00
NO 8'9	APR 7 '94	OCT 17 '96	JE 30 '00
FE 11'92	APR 20 '94	APR 02 '97	SE 06 '00
JY 10'9	JUN 23 '94	SEP 20 '9	DE 27 '00
OC 15'92	JUL 21 '94	NOV 18 '9	MY 04 '01
OC 29'9	SEP 05 '94	APR 01 '9	JY 09 01
			AG 08 '01
			AU 22 01
			FE 16 '02

EAU CLAIRE DISTRICT LIBRARY

DEMCO

I CAN BE A

RANCHER

By Kathy Henderson

CP CHILDRENS PRESS®

CHICAGO

EAU CLAIRE DISTRICT LIBRARY

80735

B+T 1/8/91 #13.22

Library of Congress Cataloging-in-Publication Data

Henderson, Kathy, 1949-
  I can be a rancher / by Kathy Henderson.
     p.   cm.
  Summary: Discusses the work done by ranchers, the
kind of skills and training they need, and the types of
animals they frequently raise.
  ISBN 0-516-01962-7
  1.   Ranchers—Vocational guidance—Juvenile
literature.   2.   Ranch life—Juvenile literature.
[1.   Ranchers—Vocational guidance.   2.   Ranch life.
3.   Occupations.   4.   Vocational guidance.]   I.   Title.
SF80.H46   1990
636'.0023—dc20   90-37678
                                                          CIP
                                                           AC

To Karen and Ralph Walchle,
for their help and generosity

Copyright © 1990 by Childrens Press®, Inc.
All rights reserved. Published simultaneously in Canada.
Printed in the United States of America.
1 2 3 4 5 6 7 8 9 10 R 99 98 97 96 95 94 93 92 91 90

PICTURE DICTIONARY

mountains

corrals

ranch

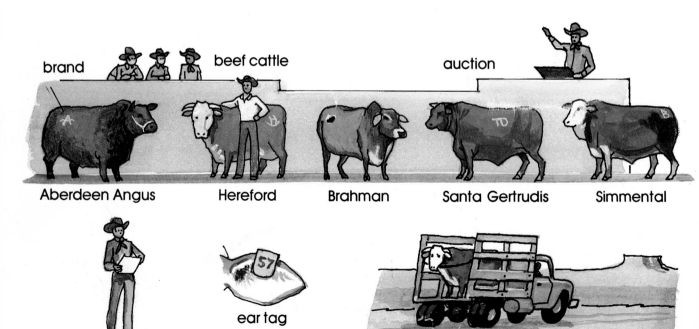

brand   beef cattle   auction

Aberdeen Angus   Hereford   Brahman   Santa Gertrudis   Simmental

rancher   ear tag   rustlers

dairy cattle

Holsteins   calves

buffalo

llamas

drought

foals   horses

elk

lambs   sheep

flood

helicopters

prairie grass

flatlands

pastures

round up

rodeo

salt
blocks

vaccines

agricultural college

all-terrain vehicles

computer

Cattle (above) and horses (below) are raised on ranches.
Ranch hands on horseback take care of the herds.

Buffalo round up in South Dakota

Sheep and pigs in a pasture in Canada

Some ranchers raise unusual animals like buffalo, elk, or llamas. Some ranchers raise horses. Many ranchers raise sheep. But most ranchers raise beef cattle.

Ranch animals are grazers. They eat grass day after day. They need lots of room to roam so that they can always find new grass to eat.

buffalo

elk

llamas

foals   horses

lambs   sheep

prairie grass

rancher

5

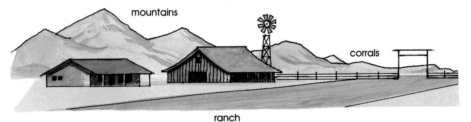

Many ranches are large.
They may cover several
thousand acres of land.
Some large ranches are
located near mountains.
Their pastures reach far
up the mountain slopes.
Other ranches are spread

flatlands

pastures

across miles of dry, flat
land where hardly
anything grows except
wild prairie grass.

It may take a rancher
several days to travel on
horseback from one end
of the ranch to the other.

These Hereford cattle on a ranch in Montana will be moved to another pasture when they have eaten up the grass on this pasture.

Ranchers must know how many animals their land can support. If a rancher has too many animals, the land will become overgrazed. There will not be enough grass for all the animals.

Overgrazing also hurts
the land, making it hard
for new grass to grow.

Drought and floods can
damage the land too.
Sometimes, when there is
not enough food for the
animals, ranchers are
forced to sell, or market,

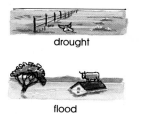
drought

flood

Left: Drought caused this pond to shrink. Right: Ranchers look at grazed and ungrazed pastures. The ungrazed land is to the left of the fence.

their animals early. Because the animals weigh less, the rancher gets less money.

Ranchers must know what types of animals can be raised on their land. Beef cattle are

brand   beef cattle

Aberdeen Angus   Hereford

Left: Hereford cattle on the range. The windmill pumps water for the cattle. Right: Aberdeen Angus cattle.

Cows are milked by machines run by computers (left). The Holstein dairy cow (right) gives more milk than other breeds.

raised for their meat. Dairy cattle are raised for their milk. The most popular breeds of beef cattle are Aberdeen Angus and Hereford. Holsteins are a breed of dairy cows.

dairy cattle

Holsteins   calves

Left: Brahman cattle have droopy ears and a hump on their shoulders. Right: A Simmental bull.

Simmentals originally came from Switzerland. They are sure-footed animals and thrive well in steep mountain regions.

In hot climates, many cattle ranchers prefer purebred or crossbred Brahmans. Brahmans are

Brahman   Santa Gertrudis   Simmental

EAU CLAIRE DISTRICT LIBRARY

related to the large-humped Zebu of India.

The cherry-red Santa Gertrudis is also popular in hot climates. This breed was developed in the early 1900s at the King Ranch in southern Texas.

Shorthorn cattle and Brahmans were crossbred to develop the Santa Gertrudis. The calves grow rapidly.

Ranch workers take care of the animals. An ingrown horn is removed from a cow (top left). A horse gets a new shoe (bottom left). Hay is brought down from the loft for the animals (above).

Even though ranch animals graze for food, there is a lot of work for ranchers to do all year round.

In early spring, calves, foals, and lambs are born. They are given vaccines to help prevent diseases like pneumonia or scours, a form of diarrhea. They

calves

vaccines

foals

lambs

A newborn calf is cleaned by its mother.

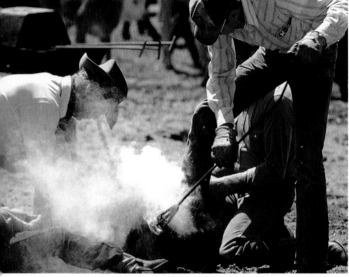

A hot iron is used to burn a mark called a brand into a calf's skin (left). These Hereford calves can be identified by their ear tags (right).

brand

ear tag

are also marked with the rancher's special brand, tattoo, or ear tag. This mark helps identify them if they are stolen by cattle thieves—sometimes called rustlers—or if they get mixed up with someone else's herd. Ranch animals are also treated with pesticides to control flies and internal worms.

Cattle are sprayed to kill ticks and fleas (left). A cow is treated by mouth for internal worms (right).

Sheep are sheared with electric clippers (left). The sheep will grow a new coat.

Sheep have their heavy winter coats clipped off.

In late spring, ranchers round up their herds and move them to different pastures to graze. The ranchers check that there

round up

is enough grass and water available for all the animals. They put out salt blocks mixed with other minerals for the animals to lick. The animals need these minerals to stay healthy.

salt blocks

A water supply is very important for ranching. Water is scarce in the western states where many ranches are located.

Ranchers on horseback move cattle to another pasture.

Every three or four weeks, as the grass in one pasture is eaten up, the ranchers move the animals to pastures farther away from the ranch house.

Some ranchers ride
horses to drive their herds
from pasture to pasture.
But many ranchers use
jeeps or four-wheel-drive,
all-terrain vehicles (ATVs).

all-terrain vehicles

All-terrain vehicles (right) are useful on the open range.
But horses (right) are still used for many jobs on a ranch.

A helicopter (left) is used to round up cattle. Ranchers on horseback (right) use a rope to catch a calf for branding.

helicopters

Some even use helicopters. But horses are still best for rounding up strays in thick brush and for roping cattle to be branded. For fun, ranchers often display their riding and roping skills at local rodeos.

rodeo

By fall, the grass in the lower pastures has grown again. Animals are then rounded up and driven back toward the ranch house, pasture by pasture.

In a roundup, the cattle are gathered into a herd so that they can be moved to another pasture.

Cattle are kept in pens called feedlots (left) and fattened on grain before they are sold. At the stockyards (right) the cattle are killed and made into meat.

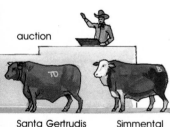

auction

Santa Gertrudis   Simmental

Healthy beef cattle that have reached market weight are shipped in trucks to be sold at an auction.

During the winter, the rest of the herd are kept in smaller pastures or corrals near the ranch house. This makes it easier for ranchers to check on the cattle. The animals may need extra feed, like hay, especially when blizzards cover the pastures with deep snow.

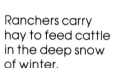

corrals

Ranchers carry hay to feed cattle in the deep snow of winter.

Most ranchers learn
their jobs by growing up
on ranches or by working
as ranch hands. Some

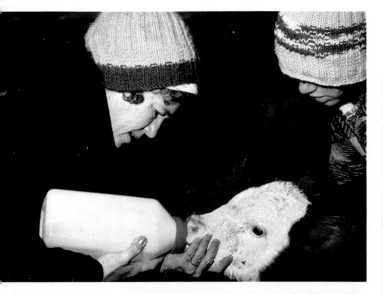

Feeding a sick calf (top left). A rancher's son learns to put a bridle on a horse (bottom left). Cattle are kept in wooden pens (below).

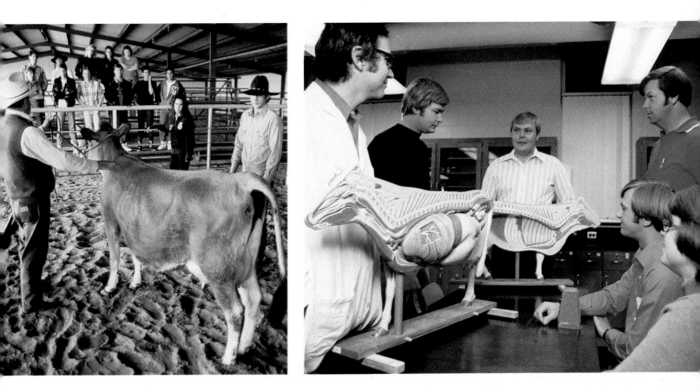

High-school students in ranching country learn about cattle (left). An agricultural-college teacher uses a model to show a cow's insides (right).

agricultural college

ranchers go to
agricultural college to
study animal science and
reproduction. Every

rancher must also know how to keep many kinds of records. Some use computers to help track expenses and sales, and to keep breeding records.

computer

Ranchers must keep careful breeding records for their animals. Many now use computers (right) to help in record keeping.

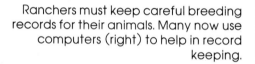

Would you like to live in the country and raise animals like sheep and horses and cattle? Then maybe you would like to be a rancher.

Grooming cattle. The people are brushing and cleaning the animal's coat.

WORDS YOU SHOULD KNOW

Aberdeen Angus(AB • er • deen ANG • guss) —
an all-black breed of beef cattle

all-terrain vehicles(AWL • ter • RAYN VEE • ih •
kilz) —vehicles that can go where there are no
roads

auction(AWK • shun) —a sale at which each
thing is sold to the person who will pay the
highest price

Brahman(BRAH • min) —a breed of cattle that
has a hump on the shoulders

buffalo(BUF • ah • loh) —a large, hoofed animal
with short horns and a humped back

corral(kor • RAL) —a fenced-in area where
horses or cattle are kept

drought(DROWT) —a time when little or no rain
falls and the grass and earth dry up

elk(EHLK) —a large deer

foal(FOHL) —a baby horse; a horse under one
year old

graze(GRAYZE) —to eat grass

Hereford(HER • ferd) —a breed of beef cattle with a reddish-brown coat and a white face

Holstein(HOLE • styne) —a black-and-white breed of dairy cow

llama(LAHMA) —an animal like a camel but smaller and without a hump

minerals(MIN • er • elz) —substances that animals need in their diet for good health

overgrazing(oh • ver • GRAY • zing) —eating too much of the grass in an area so that the grass will not grow back

pasture(PASS • cher) —a field planted with grasses for animals to eat

pesticides(PESS • tih • sides) —sprays or powders that kill pests such as fleas and ticks

Santa Gertrudis(SAN • ta ger • TROO • diss) —a reddish-colored breed of beef cattle

Simmental(SIM • in • tahl) —a sure-footed breed of beef cattle from Switzerland

vaccine(vak • SEEN) —a substance given to animals to help them fight off disease

PHOTO CREDITS

American Simmental Association—12 (right)

© Cameramann International, Ltd.—6 (left), 10 (left), 17 (right), 18 (left), 21 (right), 27 (both photos), 28 (left)

Journalism Services:
© Tim McCabe—8

Norma Morrison—18 (right)

Root Resources:
© Bill Barksdale—10 (right), 12 (left), 24 (left), 26 (bottom left), 28 (right)
© Kohout Productions—20
© Betty Kubis—4 (bottom)
© Garry D. McMichael—9 (left), 15, 25, 26 (top left)

Santa Gertruda Breeders International—13

Tom Stack and Associates:
© Byron Augustin—17 (left)
© Matt Bradley—24 (right)
© Bill Everitt—16 (left)
© Stewart M. Green—Cover
© Joe McDonald—11 (right)
© Brian Parker—11 (left)
© Bob Pool—14 (right)
© Tom Stack—21 (left)
© Spencer Swanger—6 (right)
© Jack Swenson—9 (right)
© Don and Pat Valenti—14 (bottom left)

TSW, Click/Chicago Ltd.:
© Robert Frerck—4 (top), 19
© George Hunter—5 (right)
© Zigy Kaluzny—22 (left)
© Martin Rogers—26 (right)

Third Coast Stock Source:
© Kent Knudson—22 (right)
© Mike Slater—7 (right)

Valan Photos:
© Kennon Cooke—1
© Jeff Foott—5 (left), 7 (left)
© Stephen J. Krasemann—23
© Mildred McPher—29
© Tom W. Parkin—14 (top left)
© Wayne Shiels—16 (right)

INDEX

About the Author

Kathy Henderson is Executive Director of the National Association for Young Writers, vice president of the NAYW Board of Trustees, and Michigan Advisor for the Society of Children's Book Writers. She works closely with children, teachers, and librarians through young author conferences and workshops, and is a frequent guest speaker in schools. An experienced freelance writer with hundreds of newspaper and magazine articles to her credit, she is also the author of the *Market Guide for Young Writers*. Mrs. Henderson lives on a 400-acre dairy farm in Michigan with her husband Keith, and two teenage children.